YEMEK

[Eating]

For Zoé and Tjade

Isabel Lezmi, Lisa Rienermann,
and Veronika Helvacıoğlu

YEMEK

[Eating]

Recipes from Istanbul

weldonowen

Contents

Evening

Night

A book like a day off

When it comes to Istanbul, our hearts live in our taste buds! This bustling city on the Bosporus River is unmatched in its wealth of flavors. We can no longer keep the secret to ourselves—there is a world beyond the gyro kebab!

We dove into the sea of delicacies, bathed in yogurt sauces, fished for the best Turkish pizza, and tracked sweets and treats from morning till night. From these explorations has emerged a book that's something like a vacation day: it starts gently with breakfast (with copious draughts of tea), is closely followed by a relaxed lunch, glides into a sweet teatime followed by the luxurious dishes of dinner, and is rounded off with wondrous midnight snacks. On our journey we found amazing recipes and encountered wonderful people, all of which we bring to you on the following pages along with descriptions of typical Turkish ingredients (from eggplants to olives) and culinary tales of chicken pudding and lion's milk.

Whether a fluffy olive bake, homemade mini tortellini in yogurt sauce, sweet carrot squares, bean purée, zucchini cream, or red lentil soup, most of these recipes are extremely easy to cook. We have dipped deep into our favorites, those recipes where our hearts linger. Vegan, vegetarian, and gluten-free recipes are all noted, and when a Turkish ingredient may be difficult to find, there's a glossary at the end of the book that suggests possible substitutions.

In these pages, we hope you will find more than just a tasty recipe, and we wish you *afiyet olsun*—enjoy!

Isabel, Lisa & Veronika

East meets West in Istanbul, Turkey's capital city.

MORNING

[sabah]

A delicious start

Günaydın (good morning)! Let's head right into *kahvaltı*, the savory Turkish breakfast. Olives and feta cheese greet the newly awakened, accompanied by *simit* (sesame rings) or freshly baked bread, torn into pieces and served with strong black çay (tea).

On weekends, the people of Istanbul make their way to the Sarıyer District, on the European side of this ancient city, where there are many breakfast cafes on the shores of the Bosporus River. Overlooking the crowded promenade, the cafes serve breakfast until the afternoon. Friendly waiters deliver delicious plates of fried eggs with *sucuk*, the local garlic sausage, as well as other local favorites. After breakfast has been savored, it's onward into the day—*haydi bakalım* (come along then)!

menemen

Scrambled Eggs with Vegetables

serves 4

vegetarian + gluten-free

Time
about 20 minutes

Ingredients
1 large tomato
2 green bell peppers
¼ lb garlic sausage (optional)
4 green onions
3 stalks parsley
2 Tbsp butter
1 Tbsp bell pepper paste
5 eggs
1.5 oz feta cheese
1 tsp red pepper flakes
salt
pepper

Goes well with
freshly baked white bread
and olives

Tip
Use eggplant instead
of bell peppers.

We'll get straight to the point: *menemen* is the perfect hangover breakfast (especially if you have someone who makes it for you). But even without a sore head, it's still a great dish!

Bring a large pot of water to a boil and remove from the stove. Using a sharp knife, cut a shallow X in the bottom of the tomato and place the tomato in the hot water. Remove the tomato with a slotted spoon after 1–2 minutes and let cool on a plate. Then peel off the skin with a knife.

Dice the tomato finely. Wash the bell peppers, remove the seeds and chop finely. Cut the green onions into thin rings. Chop the parsley finely and set aside.

Melt the butter in a large pan over medium heat. Add the peppers and garlic sausage, if using, and sauté for 2 minutes. Add the green onions and bell pepper paste and sauté briefly. Add the diced tomato to the pan, reduce the heat and simmer for about 5 minutes until the liquid has been reduced.

Crack the eggs into a bowl and beat with a whisk. Move the vegetables to one side of the pan with a wooden spoon and add the beaten eggs. Stir slowly with a wooden spoon or spatula over low heat, bringing in the egg mixture from the sides of the pan. Stir in the vegetables and remove the pan from the heat.

Crumble the feta onto the scrambled eggs and vegetables. Scatter parsley and pepper flakes on top and season with salt and pepper.

sürmelik

Breakfast Spreads

A Turkish breakfast includes all kinds of cheese, olives, and egg dishes and, in general, is salty. However, there are many sparkling highlights for the sweet-toothed. Here are our three favorite sweet spreads.

---

tahin pekmez / Sesame Paste & Grape Molasses

serves 4

vegan + gluten-free

Time about 5 minutes

Ingredients
2½ Tbsp grape molasses
2½ Tbsp tahini

Simply stir the two ingredients together in a small bowl and pour into a small jar. If the tahini is rather thick, shake the jar or stir with a fork to mix the tahini with the molasses. Taste the paste and adjust the seasoning; some prefer a nuttier taste while others like it a touch sweeter; if you prefer a sweeter flavor add more molasses. We like the 50-50 mix!

---

incir marmelatı / Fig Jam

makes about 3-4 jam jars

vegetarian + gluten-free

Time about 20 minutes

Ingredients
18 medium or 24 small figs
2½ cups preserving sugar
½ tsp aniseed (optional)

Wash the figs and cut into quarters. Put in a large pot, add the preserving sugar and, if using, the anise seed. Bring to a boil and let cook for about 3 minutes, stirring occasionally with a wooden spoon. Fill right to the top into sterilized jam jars and cover.

---

bal kaymak / Honey & Cream

serves 4

Time 5 minutes

Ingredients
1 cup clotted cream
about 8-10 Tbsp honey
fresh loaf of white bread

Place the cream in equal portions onto four small breakfast plates and pour about 2-3 tablespoons honey over each portion. Serve with slices of fresh bread.

The first cup of tea of the day by the Bosporus —
it's going to be a GREAT day!

Twenty Teas and One Coffee

Steaming tulip glasses and foaming pots

The Turks drink çay, black tea, very hot and very strong. This steaming wake-up call is served in gold-edged tulip glasses that tinkle brightly as you stir in the obligatory and generous amount of sugar with the small ornate silver spoon.

Turkish black tea is made in a *demlik*, a container with two parts: a small teapot in which loose black tea leaves are brewed, sitting atop a larger pot containing hot water. The perfect cup of çay consists of one-third of brewed tea topped with hot water from the lower container. Those who like weaker tea order *açık*: less tea, and more water, in the tulip-shaped glass.

To take tea in Istanbul (and indeed, in all of Turkey) is a daily ritual and always a gesture of hospitality. Whether you're in a real estate office, at the hairdresser's, or with a neighbor, one thing is certain: to refuse tea is impolite. So stop counting and drink it whenever it's offered.

By the way, a çaycı takes care of the regular refills. Every business (it doesn't matter if it's a bank, a workshop, or an office) has someone who's responsible for providing tea (a bit like the English "tea lady"!). And if they don't, there's always a tea shop around the corner whose busy employees make their way through the street balancing trays of steaming glasses of tea.

Sip and savor!

Don't feel like tea? There is always *türk kahvesi*, Turkish coffee. Although not drunk or offered as often as tea, it is really quite special. It is prepared in a small side-handled pot made from stainless steel, brass, or copper. You have to specify your desired sweetness when you order: *sade* (plain black), *az şekerli* (a little sugar), *orta* (sweeter), or *şekerli* (spoon stands up). When the brown gold arrives, don't stir it—the grounds will swirl up.

Türk kahvesi is drunk from small, richly decorated porcelain cups. Leave a bit behind or you'll get a mouthful of grounds. You read the future from the residue left in the cup... Cover the cup with its saucer and give it a shake. When the grounds are dry, you can make out shapes and figures that will give you a hint about your fate.

türk kahvesi / Turkish Coffee

serves 4

Time 5 minutes

Ingredients
8 tsp Turkish coffee
sugar to taste

Place the coffee and sugar to taste in a small pot (cezve) over low heat and add four coffee cups of water. Bring to a boil, stirring continuously.

As soon as some foam begins to develop, skim it off with a small spoon and distribute it equally among four coffee cups. Bring the coffee to a boil over low heat a second time and pour into the cups.

Drink the coffee when the grounds have settled at the bottom of the cups.

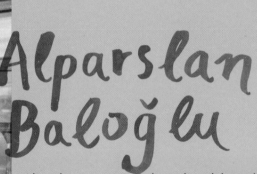

Alparslan Baloğlu

Alparslan is a gourmet through and through. He loves fresh fish at the *kıyı* on the Bosporus, a long-standing establishment with a seasonal menu and views of the strait, just as much as he likes a simple *nohutlu pilav* (rice with chickpeas or chicken) from a stall on the street—and never without his own special ingredient: small green peppers fresh from the garden! He always carries a small bag of these in his trouser pocket and has some with every meal to add a touch of heat. His favorite hobby is to make preserves, on which he spares no effort. His walnut preserve takes forever to make, but even in fast-paced Istanbul, true connoisseurs have a liking for slow food.

ceviz macunu / Black Walnut Preserve

makes about 8–9 jam jars

vegan + gluten-free

Time
about 90 minutes
(+ 9 days for resting)

Ingredients
about 4½ lb green walnuts
about 4½ lb sugar
3 tsp cloves
juice of 1 lemon

The best time to pick green walnuts is at the end of June, before the shells have time to harden.

Peel the walnuts with a small sharp knife, wearing disposable gloves as the nuts will stain your skin. Put the nuts in a large pot and cover with water. Let stand overnight. The next day, drain off the dark brown water and cover the nuts with fresh water. Repeat this process for 8 days.

On the last day, drain the nuts in a colander and wash thoroughly under running cold water. Put the nuts in a pot with boiling water and simmer for 15 minutes. Drain, rinse with cold water and let dry. Put the nuts back into the pot and add the sugar. Let stand overnight. The next day, add 2 cups of water and the cloves, bring to a boil, and simmer for 30 minutes. Add the lemon juice and simmer for another 10 minutes. Let cool, then pour into sterilized jam jars.

Poğaça

Feta & Dill Rolls

makes about 10 rolls

vegetarian

Time
about 40 minutes
(+ 30 minutes for resting and
about 45 minutes for baking)

Ingredients
3 cups flour
1 tsp salt
1½ tsp baking powder
½ cup cold butter
3 eggs
7 Tbsp olive oil
¾ cup plain whole-milk yogurt
½ cup fresh dill, chopped
about ½ cup feta cheese
2 Tbsp fresh mint, chopped
  (optional)
2 tsp milk
2 tsp sesame seeds
2 tsp black cumin seeds

Poğaça is the only Turkish word that Veronika cannot pronounce correctly, even after ten years in Istanbul. Her love for these stuffed herbed rolls sprinkled with seeds is not diminished by her inability to say their name.

Combine the flour, salt, and baking powder in a large bowl. Cut the butter into small pieces and add to the bowl. Mix the ingredients with your hands or an electric handheld mixer. Add 2 eggs, the oil, yogurt, and dill and knead well until you get a smooth dough.

Shape the dough into a ball, cover with plastic wrap, and put in the fridge for 30 minutes.

Take out the dough, remove the plastic wrap, and cut the dough into two equal halves. Shape each half into a 6-inch-long roll. Cut each roll into 5 equal pieces and transfer to a baking sheet lined with parchment paper.

Preheat the oven to 375°F.

Flatten the dough pieces with your hands into oval shapes about ½ inch thick. Put some feta and fresh mint, if using, on one half of each oval, leaving a ½-inch border. Fold the other half of the oval over the filling, press the edges together tightly, and fold the edges over a bit so that the cheese doesn't spill out.

Whisk the last egg with the milk in a small bowl and brush on top of each roll. Sprinkle with sesame seeds and/or black cumin seeds and place on the middle rack in the oven. Bake for about 45 minutes.

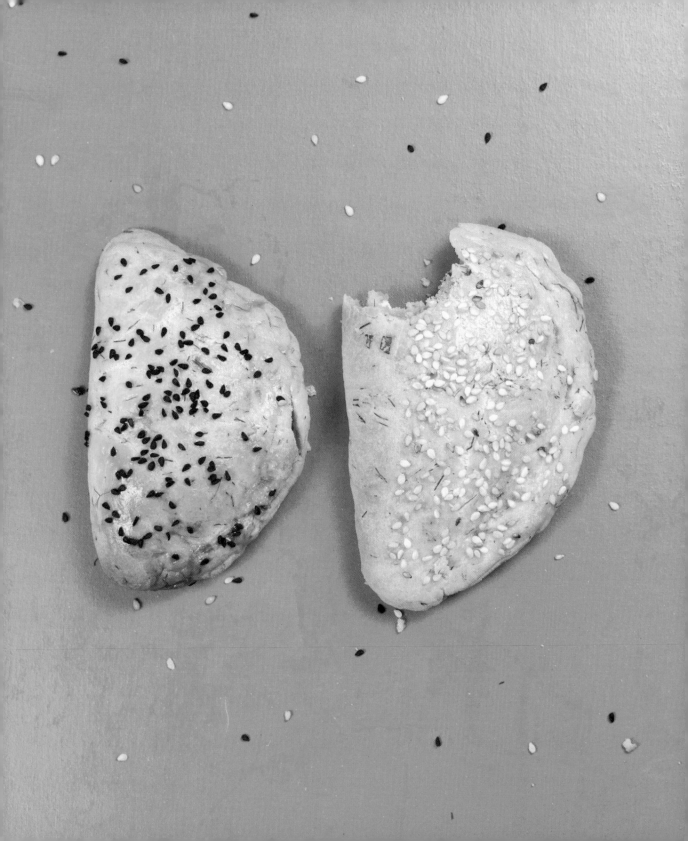

FİLE
1
T.L

A Sunday market in the Tarlabaşı district

Olives

Turkey is one of the world's
largest producers of olives, with
almost 100 million olive trees
under cultivation. Many are several
hundred years old and some have
seen their thousandth birthday.

Whether pink, light green, or black, the color reveals not
the variety but the olives' ripeness. The earlier the
harvest, the lighter the color and the firmer the texture,
and the little more bitter the taste than their dark
brethren that have had more time to ripen on the tree.

Olives are usually pierced to make it
easier to remove the pit. Our motto
is: let's get to the taste faster!

You can tell good black olives by
their pit: a light brown pit means
that the olive has ripened naturally;
a dark brown pit indicates that
coloring has been added.

The best-known Turkish variety is called *gemlik*.
It is black and a bit wrinkled, and is often
pressed to make olive oil. For 3½ cups of oil
you need 10½ lbs of olives.

zeytin ezmeli açma

Sweet Bagels with Olive Paste

makes about 10 bagels

vegetarian

Time
about 50 minutes
(+ 45 minutes for resting)

Ingredients
1½ milk
1 tsp superfine sugar

1 cube fresh active yeast
½ cup butter
1½ lb flour
1 tsp salt
4 Tbsp granulated sugar
1 beaten egg
10-12 tsp olive paste
olive oil
1 egg yolk
2 tsp black cumin seeds

Olive paste *(zeytin ezmesi)* is a must at every Turkish breakfast table. You can buy it or make it yourself (see recipe, page 155). It tastes particularly good in these sweet bagels.

Pour ½ cup milk in a pot and heat until tepid. Remove from the heat, add the superfine sugar and the yeast, stirring until it has dissolved. Dice the butter and add to the milk. Let the mixture cool slightly. Combine the flour, salt, and sugar in a large bowl. Add the beaten egg, the remaining milk and the milk, yeast, and butter mixture.

Mix the ingredients to a smooth dough. If it is too sticky, add a bit of flour. If it is too crumbly, add a bit of milk. Shape the dough into a ball, cover the bowl with a clean kitchen towel and proof the dough for 45 minutes.

Preheat the oven to 475°F and place a rack in the middle of the oven. Dust a work surface with flour to shape the *açma*: Divide the dough into 10 equal balls and shape each ball into a flat rectangle about 12 inches long by 3 inches wide and ½ inch thick. With a brush or small knife, brush olive paste onto each piece of dough, leaving a border of approximately ½ inch. If the olive paste is too firm, mix a little bit of oil into it.

Roll up each piece of dough from the longer side, then shape it into a ring and press the ends together firmly. Place the rings on a baking sheet lined with parchment paper. Brush each ring with egg yolk and sprinkle with black cumin seeds.

Place the baking sheet on the middle rack of the oven and bake for about 10–15 minutes.

pazarlıklar

Kekik belongs to the mint family and tastes similar to thyme and oregano. It's delicious with meat!

Black cumin seeds *(çörek otu)* are sprinkled over baked goods such as flatbread for an aromatic note.

Pul biber is a paprika seasoning that is available with different levels of heat. In its mildest form it's almost sweet.

The tart and sour sumac *(sumak)* is made from the dried fruit of the staghorn sumac tree. It is often sprinkled on raw onions and served with meat.

Figs *(incir)* are plentiful in August and September. They are perfectly ripened when a small drop of honey hangs from their lower opening.

Kelek, a small unripened melon, looks like a cocoa bean and tastes like a particularly sweet and crunchy cucumber.

Unripe plums *(erik)* are edible heralds of spring that are delightful sprinkled with salt.

Sugary sweet mulberries *(kara dut)* appear in summer in dark violet and white. (See page 60.)

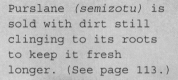

Purslane *(semizotu)* is sold with dirt still clinging to its roots to keep it fresh longer. (See page 113.)

Wild thyme *(taze kekik)* tastes fantastic in a salad.

Artichoke hearts *(enginar)* are found in Turkish markets freshly peeled and soaking in lemon water to keep them from going brown.

Turkish basil *(fesleğen)* has small leaves and is sold in pots.

Yenidünya are related to medlars and taste refreshingly sour.

The sea vegetable samphire *(deniz börülcesi)* goes well with fish. (See page 118.)

Pomegranate *(nar)* seeds are great as freshly pressed juice or in salads. (See page 43.)

Roka is Turkish large-leaved arugula.

Çiriş is an aromatic cousin of asparagus.

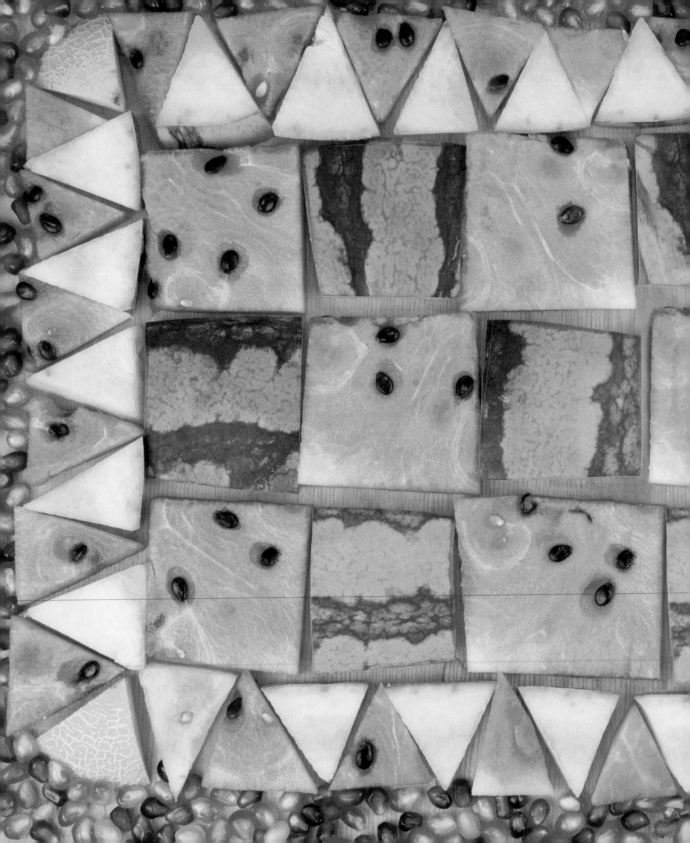

MIdDAY

[öğlen]

BEYOND KEBABS

Once they have finished their walk through the must-see Sultanahmet quarter, with its palaces and bazaars, every visitor to the city will need a replenishing lunch. It could be *mantı*, the Turkish tortellini, or *mahmudiye*, a chicken and apricot stew.

Those still digesting breakfast will want something lighter. Stop at one of the many street-food stalls and try a delicious fish roll or hearty meat sandwich along with ice-cold watermelon or grilled corn on the cob. So simple, sooo good!

Turkish Tortellini

serves 4

vegetarian

Time
about 2 hours
(+ 1 hour for resting)

Ingredients
2¼ cups flour
1 egg
salt
1 small onion
1 Tbsp olive oil
2 sprigs parsley
3 medium potatoes, boiled
½ tsp red pepper flakes
1¾ cups full-fat yogurt
1 garlic clove
2 Tbsp butter
1 Tbsp paprika paste

For serving
sumac
dried mint
red pepper flakes
chopped walnuts

Tip
The more people helping with preparing and folding the tortellini, the quicker the *mantı* will be ready to eat!

In almost every Turkish supermarket you will find ready-made *mantı*. Most are filled with meat and are delicious. But we prefer to make our own—with a vegetarian potato filling.

Put the flour, egg, about ½ cup water and ½ teaspoon salt in a large bowl, combine thoroughly and knead with your hands or an electric handheld mixer to a smooth dough. Shape into ball. Cover the bowl with a clean, wet kitchen towel and let the dough rest in the bowl for about 1 hour.

For the filling, dice the onion finely and sauté in the oil in a small pan until slightly golden. Chop the parsley finely. Mash the boiled potatoes in a medium bowl and mix in the parsley, pepper flakes, and onion. Season with salt and set aside.

Halve the dough. Roll out one half on a floured work surface as thin as possible. Cut the rolled-out dough into 1¼ by 1¼-inch squares.

Put ½ teaspoon of filling in the middle of each square. Fold the facing corners of the square over the filling and press firmly together so that you get a small pouch (see folded and cooked *mantı* on page 34). Press tightly to seal the edges so that the *mantı* don't split open when you cook them.

Repeat with the second half of dough. Bring a large pot of salted water to a boil, add the *mantı*, and boil over medium heat for 12–14 minutes. Drain in a colander.

Put the yogurt in bowl. Peel and crush the garlic and add to the yogurt, add salt to taste, and stir well. Set aside. Melt the butter in a small pan over low heat and add the paprika paste. Stir and pour into a small jug.

Place the *mantı* in deep bowls. Pour over the yogurt sauce and drizzle with the paprika butter. Serve with sumac, dried mint, pepper flakes, and chopped walnuts in small bowls for each diner to season the *mantı* the way he or she likes.

kavun dolması

Baked Melon with Rice, Nuts & Spices

serves 4

gluten-free

Time
about 1 hour

Ingredients
2 Galia melons
1¾ cup rice
2 onions
2 garlic cloves
2 cardamom pods
4 Tbsp sunflower oil
14 oz ground beef
2 Tbsp pomegranate syrup
3 Tbsp currants
4 Tbsp walnuts, chopped
2 oz pine nuts
2 oz shelled pistachios
3 tsp red pepper flakes
pinch ground cumin
½ tsp sumac
1 tsp black cumin seeds
1 tsp dried mint
pinch ground cinnamon
1 Tbsp lemon juice
salt
pepper
about 2 Tbsp butter
1 Tbsp honey
1–2 tsp fresh mint, chopped
1–2 tsp fresh parsley,
  chopped

In the Fatih district, the restaurant Asitane has a special theme: the preparation of Ottoman dishes characteristic of a sultan's palace kitchen. This stuffed melon, inspired by one on Asitane's menu, looks so wonderful that we could easily imagine ourselves at a sultan's banquet.

With a sharp knife cut the melons horizontally in a zigzag pattern. Remove the seeds. Using a teaspoon, scoop out half the flesh in small balls and put them in a bowl. Set aside the melon halves and melon balls.

Cook the rice according to the directions on the package, drain, and set aside. Peel the onions and the garlic and chop finely. Open the cardamom pods, remove the seeds, and grind them finely using a mortar and pestle.

Heat the sunflower oil in a large pan over medium heat, add the onions and garlic and sauté until golden. Add the ground beef, stirring frequently, and fry until brown and crumbly.

Add the pomegranate syrup, currants, and the nuts and stir. Add 1 tsp pepper flakes, cumin, sumac, cumin seeds, dried mint, cinnamon, and cardamom. Season with lemon juice, salt, and pepper.

Heat the oven to 350°F. Add the cooked rice to the meat and stir to mix well. Fill each melon half with about a quarter of the mixture. Place the melon halves on a baking sheet lined with parchment paper and bake on the middle rack for 25 minutes.

Heat the butter in a pan over medium heat and quickly sauté the melon balls. Drizzle the honey over the melon balls and sprinkle with the remaining 2 teaspoons pepper flakes and 2 pinches of salt.

Remove the melons from the oven. Sprinkle with mint and parsley and serve with the spicy melon and butter sauce.

When it's hot outside,
a plate of watermelon makes
a wonderful lunch!

Pomegranates

A pomegranate contains up to 400 seeds. Each seed is covered with brilliant red flesh and looks like a small ruby.

The pink outer skin of the pomegranate is extremely robust. It keeps in the fridge for weeks. It's in season from September through December.

The best way to remove pomegranate seeds is in a large bowl of water. Cut the pomegranate in half, put the halves in water, and remove the seeds; this method prevents the juice from spraying.

Freshly pressed pomegranate juice can be a sour business. The juice stores of Istanbul will often mix it with orange or carrot juice to take the edge off it. These are real vitamin bombs!

Nar ekşisi is a delicious sweet-and-sour pomegranate syrup (see page 59). The syrup is especially good in salad dressings and meat marinades.

buğday salatası

Wheat, Feta & Pomegranate Salad

serves 4

vegetarian

Time
about 30 minutes
(+ soaking overnight)

Ingredients
1 cup dried black-eyed peas
2 cups whole wheat
salt
8 oz feta cheese
1 pomegranate, seeds only
6 sprigs parsley, chopped
3 sprigs mint, chopped
4 Tbsp walnuts, chopped
5 Tbsp olive oil
1 tsp lemon juice
2 tsp pomegranate syrup
pepper
1 tsp black cumin seeds

The Ara, a lovely cafe in Istanbul named after the famous Turkish photographer Ara Güler, makes a particularly good version of this fresh and fruity wheat, cheese, and nut salad. Making this salad at home takes time as the wheat and the black-eyed peas need to soak overnight, but that only heightens the pleasant anticipation...

Put the black-eyed peas and wheat into a large pot, cover with water and let soak overnight.

The next morning, drain off the water and cover the black-eyed peas and wheat with fresh water and salt. Bring to a boil and simmer over low heat for about 20–30 minutes until tender.

Cut the feta into bite-size pieces and put in a serving bowl together with the pomegranate seeds, herbs, and walnuts. Add the peas and wheat.

For the dressing, in a medium bowl, mix together the oil, lemon juice, and pomegranate syrup and season with salt and pepper. Pour the dressing over the salad in the bowl, toss thoroughly, and sprinkle with black cumin seeds.

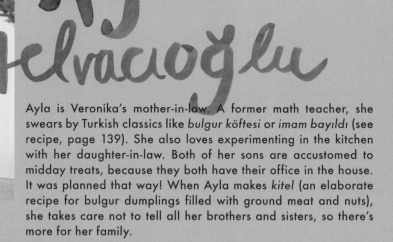

Ayla Helvacıoğlu

Ayla is Veronika's mother-in-law. A former math teacher, she swears by Turkish classics like *bulgur köftesi* or *imam bayıldı* (see recipe, page 139). She also loves experimenting in the kitchen with her daughter-in-law. Both of her sons are accustomed to midday treats, because they both have their office in the house. It was planned that way! When Ayla makes *kitel* (an elaborate recipe for bulgur dumplings filled with ground meat and nuts), she takes care not to tell all her brothers and sisters, so there's more for her family.

bulgur köftesi / Bulgur & Herb Dumplings

serves 4

vegan

Time about 1 hour
(+ 1 hour soaking time)

Ingredients
1 cup fine bulgur
1 tsp ground cumin
salt
all-purpose flour
oil
2 large tomatoes
1 tsp paprika paste
pepper
½ bunch fresh mint, chopped
½ bunch fresh parsley, chopped

Put the bulgur in a bowl, cover it with warm water, and let soak for 1 hour. Add the cumin and 1 teaspoon salt. Knead with your hands until you get a smooth mixture. If it is too sticky, add a bit of flour; if it is too dry, add more water.

With moist hands, shape the mixture into hazelnut-size dumplings. Using a finger, press an indent into the center of each dumpling and place the dumplings on a platter next to each other (in one layer, not stacked on top of each other). Set the platter aside.

Bring a large pot of water to a boil, add the dumplings, and simmer over low heat until they rise onto the surface, about 3 minutes. Drain in a colander.

Bring a large pot of water to a boil. Grate the tomatoes roughly and add to the water with the paprika paste. Season with salt and pepper. Ladle into four soup plates, add the dumplings, and sprinkle with mint and parsley.

mücver

Zucchini Fritters with Feta & Herbs

makes about 25 fritters

vegetarian

Time
about 50 minutes

Ingredients
2 large zucchini
salt
4 oz feta cheese
4 green onions
3 sprigs fresh mint
3 sprigs dill
2 eggs
2 garlic cloves
½ tsp grated peel of an
   organic lemon (optional)
¾ cup all-purpose flour
½ tsp baking powder
sunflower oil
about 1 tsp butter

Goes well with
purslane salad (see recipe,
page 113) or yogurt with
cucumber and mint (see recipe,
page 110)

Tip
Use basil instead of
dill and mint.

These fritters are often served as part of a meze (small dishes of food usually served before the main course), but sadly in a tiny size. We don't approve of this, because they are so delicious that we always want to eat more of them. Serve them with a fresh yogurt dip, and we're in zucchini seventh *mücver*-heaven!

Using the large holes of a grater, shred the zucchini roughly. Place in a colander set over a bowl, sprinkle with salt, and let drain for about 15 minutes. Squeeze out any liquid, using the back of the tablespoon and pressing the shredded zucchini against the colander.

Crumble the feta into a large bowl. Finely slice the green onions and add to the bowl. Chop the mint and dill finely and add to the bowl. Whisk the eggs in a separate bowl and add to the feta and herb mixture. Crush the garlic cloves and stir in.

Add the grated lemon peel, if using. Add the flour, baking powder, and zucchini and stir well.

Cover the bottom of a large pan generously with the oil. Add the butter and heat over medium heat. As soon as the oil is hot, spoon tablespoons of the mixture into the oil, being careful not to crowd the pan.

Fry until the fritters are golden, about 2–3 minutes on each side. Remove and drain on paper towels. Repeat until you've used up the mixture. Serve warm.

In the Hand

1,001 street-food stalls

Hot chestnuts in Gezi Park, filled mussels at the Galata Tower, and pink cotton candy in Üsküdar… Istanbul's street-food vendors ply their delicious wares everywhere. On a broad shopping street, in a tiny alley, on the ferries, in front of the mosque, or tucked into the harbor. On every corner there is something tantalizing, and each is better than the other.

Fish and Meat: Crispy white bread is filled with fish fillet or *köfte*, small meatballs. Hard-boiled offal lovers must try a *kelle* sandwich: the cheeks, brain, and tongue of a sheep are cooked, chopped finely, and seasoned. A bit less extreme and appealing to more tastes is chicken with rice and chickpeas (*tavuklu pilav*), or mussels filled with rice, raisins, and pine-nut kernels.

Fruit and Vegetables: Cucumber is the best summer street food ever! Peeled and sprinkled with salt, cucumber is the perfect refreshment when the temperature is in the high eighties. If fruit is your thing, try a portion of sliced watermelon. In winter there's grilled corn on the cob, or corn kernels in a cup with herbs and sauces of your choice.

Nuts and Chestnuts: In Istanbul, fresh hazelnuts are in season at the end of summer. They are sold in their green husks fresh from the bush. Fresh hazelnuts are no comparison to their prepacked relatives. All through Turkey, roasted chestnuts are not just a wintery treat, but are found all year. The same goes for sunflower and pumpkin seeds, which make a lovely snack for a break on a park bench or on the shores of the Bosporus.

Sweet and Sticky: Cotton candy is always bright pink, not turned at the stall but draped on a stick and carried around by the vendors. It looks amazing and makes not just kids' hearts beat a bit faster. The grown-ups go for the smaller, but just as sweet, snack called *tulumba*—fried spritz cookies dunked in sugar syrup.

*"Buyrun,
Buyuuuun!"**

Wet and Hot: In the chilly season, *boza* and *sahlep* are found at street-vendor stalls. Both are sweet hot drinks. The thick and sweet *boza* is made from fermented cereals and is a bit alcoholic. As well as sipping it, you can eat it with a spoon with cinnamon and roasted chickpeas. *Sahlep* consists of milk, plenty of sugar (of course!), and powdered wild orchid root.

*"Come and get it!" call the street vendors to passersby.

pilav / Street-Food Chicken & Rice

serves 4

gluten-free

Time
about 45 minutes

Ingredients
2 cups rice
salt
6 bay leaves
a few soup vegetables
   (such as leeks and
   carrots; optional)
4 chicken breasts
¼ cup butter
½ can chickpeas

Cook the rice according to the directions on the package. Fill another pot with water, add the salt, bay leaves, and soup vegetables and bring to a boil. Add the chicken breasts and simmer over low heat for 30 minutes. Using a slotted spoon, remove the chicken breasts and let cool. Set the stock aside.

Using your fingers and/or a sharp knife, shred the chicken finely. Stir the butter and 2–3 tablespoons of chicken stock into the cooked rice.

Drain the chickpeas in a colander. Mix the rice, chickpeas, and chicken in a large bowl. Arrange on four plates and serve.

Our favorite place
for a fish sandwich
– right by the water!

Street-food stall near the Galata Bridge

mercimek köftesi

Lemony Lentil Dumplings

makes about 60 dumplings

vegan

Time
about 20 minutes
(+ 40 minutes for
cooking and soaking)

Ingredients
1⅓ cups red lentils
¾ cup fine bulgur
1 onion, finely chopped
1 Tbsp sunflower oil
1 bunch parsley, chopped
3 Tbsp paprika paste
7 Tbsp olive oil
1 tsp red pepper flakes
juice of ½ lemon
salt
pepper
generous pinch ground cumin
1 lemon

Goes well with
firm, green salad leaves
such as romaine lettuce; use
them as an "edible napkin"

Mercimek köftesi, the slightly flattened dumplings made from red lentils, are vegan and not to be confused with traditional *çiğ köfte*. Both look similar, but the latter are made from bulgur seasoned with meat stock (see Savory Bites, page 145). Ours are much nicer!

Fill a pot with 2½ cups of water and add the lentils. Bring to a boil, reduce the heat, and simmer over low heat for about 20 minutes. Remove from the heat, stir in the bulgur, and let soak for 20 minutes.

Add the sunflower oil to a pan, add the onion, and sauté until lightly browned. Stir the parsley, paprika paste, olive oil, pepper flakes, and lemon juice into the lentil and bulgur mixture. Season with salt, pepper, and cumin.

Put a heaping tablespoon of the mixture in your hand and shape it into a small dumpling. Place the dumpling on a large plate or platter. Continue making dumplings until you've used up the mixture. Refrigerate the dumplings before serving so that the flavors can combine. Cut the lemon into quarters for squeezing over and arrange with the lentil dumplings on plates.

yoğurt çorbası

Chilled Yogurt Soup with Chickpeas & Mint

serves 4

vegetarian

Time
about 30 minutes

Ingredients
½ cup bulgur
salt
3¼ cups full-fat yogurt
1 Tbsp dried mint
2 garlic cloves
¾ can chickpeas, drained

Tip
Instead of mixing yogurt
with water, you can use
ayran, a cold yogurt drink.
If you only have mint tea
in the house, you can use the
contents of a mint teabag.

This cold soup makes for a substantial meal on a summer day. Many variations are possible: for example, with chopped radish and dill, or with chopped egg and cucumber. On really hot days we serve it with ice cubes!

Put the bulgur in a pot, cover with water, add salt, and bring to a boil. Reduce the heat to low and simmer for about 10–15 minutes. Drain any water that is left at the end and set aside to cool.

In a large bowl, whisk the yogurt with about 1 cup of cold water, adding a little at a time until the mixture is the desired thickness. Crumble the mint between your fingers and add to the mixture. Crush the garlic cloves, add to the soup, season with salt, and stir.

Add the chickpeas and bulgur and serve.

Lisa's favorite summer dish

mahmudiye yemeği

Chicken & Apricot Stew

serves 4

gluten-free

Time
about 30 minutes
(+ 40 minutes for cooking)

Ingredients
12 dried apricots
1 onion
1 Tbsp butter
8 chicken legs
2 cups chicken stock
3 Tbsp currants
2 cinnamon sticks
1 Tbsp honey
3 Tbsp unsalted almonds
salt
pepper
2 Tbsp lemon juice

Goes well with
rice or small pasta

Simple stews like this one are often found in cafes that are only open at lunchtime and serve *ev yemekleri* (everyday dishes) at good prices. Everyone who lives in Istanbul has a private tip about where to get the best lunch. Our advice: follow your nose and try it for yourself!

Put the dried apricots into a small pot. Add enough boiling water to just about cover the apricots and let soak for 15 minutes.

Peel the onion and chop finely. Melt the butter in a large pan or casserole and sauté the onion over medium heat until transparent.

Add the chicken legs and brown on all sides. Deglaze the pan with the chicken stock. Add the apricots, including the soaking liquid, and add the currants, cinnamon sticks, honey, and almonds and season with salt and pepper.

Reduce the heat to low and cook for about 40 minutes. Stir in the lemon juice before serving.

damak tadı hatırası

Ground pistachios taste good, and not just with baklava.

Pişmaniye is a kind of sesame cotton candy. (See page 60.)

Dried mulberries are a perfect handbag snack.

Nuts in honey are great in muesli or mixed with yogurt.

Sweet sesame peanuts are addictive; best to buy by the pound!

Pistachio chocolate is found in every supermarket. Our favorite kind is "*damak*."

Lokum comes beautifully packed from *Aytekin Erol* in the Asian district of Moda.

Beautiful <u>mortars and mills</u> can be found for good prices at the spice bazaar.

<u>Spices</u> are always a lovely souvenir. Some nice ones are listed on page 30.

<u>Pot mats</u> like this one are made in 1,001 variations. A wonderful souvenir, it will fit in any suitcase!

Nar ekşisi, <u>pomegranate syrup</u>, adds zing to meat, salads, and soups.

<u>Tea glasses and saucers</u> in every imaginable shape and color can be bought at Paşabahçe in Istanbul's Istiklal Caddesi shopping area.

<u>Loose tea</u> mixes are a delicious souvenir. Our tip: rose and verbena.

Really good <u>coffee</u> is sold at *Mehmet Efendi* in the *Eminönü* district. The shop is an Istanbul institution, selling coffee since 1871.

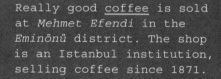

pişmaniye tatlısı

Sesame Cotton Candy with Mulberries

serves 4

Time
about 15 minutes

Ingredients
about 3½ cups full-fat yogurt
1 organic lemon
2 Tbsp superfine sugar
3¼ cups mulberries
2 Tbsp granulated sugar
about 2.2 oz *pişmaniye*
  (sesame cotton candy)

Tip
Substitute blackberries
or raspberries for
the mulberries.

Pişmaniye reminds us of cotton candy, but with a delicious overtone of sesame. *Pişmaniye* is not as sticky as its pink cousin. In this dessert, the *pişmaniye* cuts a fine figure. When preparing the plate, you must work fast or the sesame cotton candy will collapse onto itself.

Pour the yogurt into a bowl. Grate the peel of the lemon and add to the yogurt. Cut the lemon in half and squeeze the juice of one half into the yogurt. Stir well. Sift the superfine sugar into the lemon yogurt and stir. Set aside.

Rinse the mulberries and remove the long stalks. Add half the mulberries and the granulated sugar to a plastic bowl with high sides and purée with a handheld mixer. Set aside.

Divide the yogurt among four small plates. Pour the mulberry sauce into the middle. Pull off small tufts of *pişmaniye* and arrange on the sauce. Garnish with the remaining mulberries.

Midday break!

After-
noon

[öğleden sonra]

TEA
all day

Anyone who spends a day in Istanbul will have had a great deal of tea by the afternoon. It's offered everywhere, from the spice merchant while shopping at the bazaar, from the waiters on the ferry to Kadıköy, from the fish sandwich sellers at the beach stalls.

Refusing an offer of tea is considered impolite, so just relax and stir a couple of sugar cubes into your steaming tulip glass. It goes perfectly with a sweet like *cezerye* (carrot bar) and Turkish rice pudding, or with *gözleme* as a savory snack: Turkish pancakes filled with cheese and spinach. Yum!

The main thing at Istanbul teatime is to sit down. Any kind of movement with a brimming glass of hot çay is extremely unwise.

How lovely! *Hayat ne güzel!*

gözleme

Flatbread Stuffed with Spinach & Feta

serves 4

vegetarian

Time
1 hour

Ingredients
For the dough
2¼ cups whole-wheat flour
⅔ cup olive oil
1 tsp salt

For the filling
1 medium potato
2 cups spinach
2 green onions
6 oz feta, crumbled
1 tsp red pepper flakes
salt
3-4 Tbsp sunflower oil

Tip
Eggplant purée is another
truly delicious filling
for this flatbread.

Gözleme is served in many Istanbul tea gardens as a small afternoon snack. They are just right for a quick bite in between meals. Not in the mood for rolling out the dough? Then just use ready-made *yufka* dough: it works just as well! You can mix and match filling ingredients to suit your taste.

For the dough, combine the flour, olive oil, salt, and 1 cup water in a large bowl. Knead the mixture for 10 minutes until you get a sticky dough. If it is too wet, add a bit more flour. Cover the bowl with a clean kitchen towel, set aside, and let the dough rest for 20 minutes.

For the filling, peel the potato and boil in a pot of salted water until soft. Drain the potato and mash it on a deep plate with a fork, then transfer to a small bowl. Rinse the spinach, chop it finely, and place in another small bowl. Rinse the green onions, slice them finely, and place in another small bowl. Set the bowls aside.

Break off golf-ball-size bits of the dough. Dust a work surface with flour and, using a rolling pin dusted with flour, roll the dough balls into small, flat ovals with a 6-inch diameter and ¼-inch thickness.

Now for the filling. Try various combination: a bit of feta with spinach or only potatoes with pepper flakes or everything mixed together! It is important not to use too much filling as the thin dough will tear. Place the filling on the upper half of each oval, leaving a ½-inch border. Season with salt, fold the dough over the filling, and pinch the edges together. Repeat with the remaining dough and filling.

Heat the sunflower oil in large pan and fry the filled flatbread pockets over medium heat for about 2 minutes on each side until they are golden. Devour quickly: they taste best fresh from the pan!

Filled with spinach
and cheese?
Or eggplant with potatoes?
Gözleme are
always delicious!

Yufka

Yufka dough consists of flour, water, and salt.
Its secret: It must be paper thin.

To get it so thin that it's almost transparent but
still doesn't tear, you need an *oklava*. This is a
three-foot-long slim rolling pin: the traditional
tool for rolling *yufka*.

Yufka is good for all kinds of things.
It's great for sweet baklava
as well as for savory *börek*.

In Istanbul, there are many small shops,
known as *yufkacı*, producing fresh *yufka*
for sale daily. When it's fresh, it feels
wonderfully soft, like silk.

If you buy ready-made *yufka* from a
supermarket, you'll get about half
a dozen round pieces of pastry in a
package. They are large: a single
piece is about two feet in diameter!

The Turks have an lovely expression: *yufka yürekli*, or
heart of *yufka*, meaning that a person is very sensitive.

gül böreği

Savory Pastry with Potato & Feta

makes about 30 twists

vegetarian

Time
about 50 minutes
(+ 30–40 minutes for baking)

Ingredients
2 medium potatoes, boiled
¾ cup milk
½ cup butter
2 eggs
3 cups crumbled feta
2 cups Gouda cheese, grated
½ bunch parsley, chopped finely
2 Tbsp pine nuts
1 tsp red pepper flakes
salt
pepper
6 large round *yufka* sheets
  (about 24 inches in diameter)
2 Tbsp black cumin seeds

Roughly mash the boiled potatoes with a fork and set aside. Heat the milk and butter in a pot until tepid. Separate an egg and set the egg yolk aside in a bowl. Whisk the egg white and the other egg in a bowl and add the tepid milk and butter mixture, stirring. Mix the feta and Gouda with the potatoes, parsley, pine nuts, and pepper flakes. Season with salt and pepper.

Preheat the oven to 350°F.

Carefully place a *yufka* sheet on a large work surface. Tear a second *yufka* sheet into small pieces. Put the small pieces on the large sheet, leaving a border of at least 4½ inches. Place one-third of the filling on the sheet. Fold over the edges on three sides, then roll up the sheet toward the unfolded edge. Brush the unfolded edge with the milk mixture so that it will seal firmly. Finish rolling up the sheet and gently press the unfolded edge against the roll to seal it.

Cut the roll into 2-inch-wide pieces and place them with the filling facing up on a baking sheet lined with parchment paper. Repeat with the remaining *yufka* sheets and filling.

Drizzle all the rolls with the remaining milk mixture, brush with the egg yolk, and sprinkle with black cumin seeds. Bake for 30–40 minutes until the *börek* twists are lightly browned.

helva tatlısı

Sweet *Yufka* Apple Rolls

makes 15 apple rolls

Time
about 30 minutes
(+ about 30 minutes for baking)

Ingredients
2 apples
15 triangular *yufka* sheets
5 Tbsp melted butter
12 oz tahini helva
⅛ cup pine nuts
ground cinnamon (optional)
sea salt (optional)
raisins (optional)
1 cup almonds, chopped
1 Tbsp brown sugar

Goes well with
strong Turkish coffee

Tip
Instead of making small
rolls, you can shape
the buns freestyle.

This is the Turkish take on European apple strudel, made with crispy *yufka* dough, apples, and nutty *tahin helva* (sesame sweet, see page 79). It's quick to make and a sure hit with kids.

Peel and core the apples and cut into small dice. Set aside. Place one *yufka* sheet on a work surface and brush the edges with some melted butter. Crumble the *tahin helva* and sprinkle about 1 tablespoon onto the short side of the triangle. Add some apple and pine nuts. If you like, add a pinch of cinnamon, sea salt, or even some raisins.

Fold in the corners of the short side of the triangle so that the warm, melted *tahin helva* doesn't spill out and roll up towards the tip. Place the small roll on a baking sheet lined with parchment paper. Repeat the process with the remaining *yufka* sheets.

Preheat the oven to 350°F.

Brush the rolls on the baking sheet with the remaining butter and sprinkle with the chopped almonds, followed by the brown sugar.

Bake the rolls for about 30–35 minutes in the preheated oven until they are lightly golden. Let cool slightly and serve warm.

The basics of *börek*: fresh *yufka* pastry
from the Tarlabası market

tatlılar

Good-quality nuts and paper-thin pastry or angel's hair (strands of filo pastry) are the main ingredients of baklava, Turkey's beloved crunchy pastry specialty. Baklava can be made using different proportions of ingredients; layered or rolled; with pistachio (antep fıstık) or walnuts (ceviz), both classic; or experimental, with chocolate, but always with lots of sugar syrup.

Turkish white nougat comes in soft and hard varieties and is usually packed with pistachios.

Lokum (Turkish delight) means morsel and is wildly loved in Turkey. Everyone has their own favorite version of this small jellied treat, whether with almonds, hazelnuts, or pistachios.

Helva (halva) is a sweet sesame concoction and tastes particularly good with fresh lemon juice or prepared as in the recipe on page 74.

Lokum is generally covered with lots of confectioners' sugar, and until you bite into it, you won't see the colors of the flavorings like pomegranate, orange, mint, or rose. An especially tasty variation is the ginger delight from Patisserie Divan.

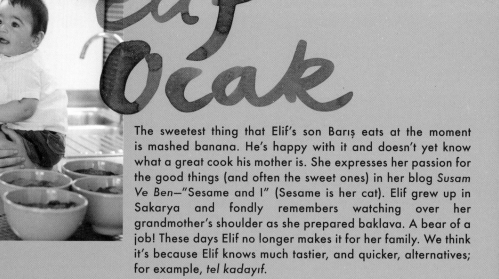

Elif Ocak

The sweetest thing that Elif's son Barış eats at the moment is mashed banana. He's happy with it and doesn't yet know what a great cook his mother is. She expresses her passion for the good things (and often the sweet ones) in her blog *Susam Ve Ben*—"Sesame and I" (Sesame is her cat). Elif grew up in Sakarya and fondly remembers watching over her grandmother's shoulder as she prepared baklava. A bear of a job! These days Elif no longer makes it for her family. We think it's because Elif knows much tastier, and quicker, alternatives; for example, *tel kadayıf*.

tel kadayıf / Angel's Hair

serves 4

Time about 20 minutes

Ingredients
⅓ cup sugar
4 Tbsp lemon juice
⅓ cup butter
6 oz *kadayıf* (strings of dough)
½ cup clotted cream
3 tsp pistachios, chopped

Goes well with
a small cup of Turkish coffee

Tip
Instead of the pistachios, use any nuts you like.

For the syrup, bring the sugar and ½ cup water to a boil in a small pot and simmer over low heat for 5 minutes. Remove from the heat, stir in the lemon juice, and let cool.

Melt the butter in another pot over low heat, remove from the heat, and let cool. Separate the string of dough with your fingers and place them on a work surface or in a shallow bowl.

Preheat the oven to 350°F. Pour the melted cooled butter over the strings of dough and knead well with your hands to distribute the butter evenly.

Put the buttered strings of dough into a 12-by-6-inch ovenproof dish, spreading them out evenly. Bake for about 40 minutes until lightly golden. Pour the cold syrup slowly over the hot *kadayıf*. With a spoon, take off four portions and arrange on small plates. Add clotted cream to taste and sprinkle with the chopped pistachios.

Tulumba—fried batter soaked in syrup—is a popular sweet snack.

Oh so sweet :
TULUMBA !

ŞEKERCİ
Aytekin Erol
CAFERZADE

www.caferzade.com.tr

KÜÇÜK
TULUMBA
KITIR - KITIR

Afiyet olsun

10 ₺

Muhallebici

A Mecca for pudding lovers

The Turks have a very special and, for some visitors, a very surprising passion: they love *muhallebi*, milk pudding. In Istanbul, there are even establishments that serve nothing but pudding. On the menu of these *muhallebici* you find *tavuk göğsü*, a hearty milk pudding with boiled and finely shredded chicken breast. This unusual dish isn't, in fact, a Turkish invention; a couple of hundred years ago this was often served in France and Italy, but only the Turks remember the secret of this ancient dish and savor it daily as if it were new.

In addition to the tourist-disturbing *tavuk göğsü* and traditional *sütlaç* (rice pudding), the classic pudding shop has other delicacies on offer. Especially delicious is *fırın sütlaç*, a mixture of rice pudding and crème brûlée, baked in the oven, which results in the pudding being covered with a fine caramel crust. A variation is *kazandibi*, a rice-flour pudding made on the stovetop rather than in the oven. For those with a taste for mastic (the dried heart of the pistachio tree), there is *sakızlı muhallebi* to try. And for the traditionalist there is *keşkül*, a simple milk and almond pudding.

Another specialty to be found in the *muhallebici*, and only made at home on special occasions, is *aşure*. In earlier times, this dish was prepared for a baby's first birthday, to celebrate his or her survival.

Aşure consists of beans, chickpeas, wheat, rice, and dried fruits and looks a little like porridge. In the shop window of the *muhallebici* it's always the best-looking pudding. Traditionally, it's decorated with pomegranate seeds, nuts, dried figs, and apricots. When fully turned out, it really steals the show from its plainer relatives (see recipe, page 86).

aşure

fırın sütlaç

Have you ever tried chicken pudding?

tavuk göğsü

fırın sütlaç /
Baked Rice Pudding

serves 4

gluten-free

Time
about 30 minutes
(+ 15–20 minutes
for baking)

Ingredients
about 4½ cups milk
⅓ cup short-grain rice
seeds of 1 vanilla pod
1½ Tbsp cornstarch
⅓ cup sugar
salt
pinch ground cinnamon
½ tsp rosewater (optional)

Put 5 tablespoons milk in a small bowl and set aside. Put the rice, vanilla seeds, and the remaining milk in a medium pot and bring to a boil. Simmer over low heat for about 25 minutes, stirring occasionally.

Preheat the oven to 375°F.

Add the cornstarch to the reserved milk in the bowl, stir well, and add to the rice mixture. Add the sugar, a generous pinch of salt, and cinnamon. Add the rosewater, if using. Raise the heat to medium and cook for about 3 minutes, stirring constantly, until the mixture thickens.

Divide the rice pudding among four small ovenproof dishes, to within about ½ inch of the rim, so that it won't spill over while baking. Bake on the top rack of the oven for 15–20 minutes. Serve warm.

aşure

Wheat Pudding with Nuts & Fruit

serves 8

vegetarian

Time
about 80 minutes
(+ 1 hour cooking time
and soaking overnight)

Ingredients
6 Tbsp spelt
2 Tbsp dried chickpeas
2 Tbsp dried white beans
2 dried figs
4 dried apricots
2 Tbsp raisins
1 cinnamon stick
4 cloves
6 Tbsp milk
1 pear
1 apple
½ cup walnuts
½ cup chestnuts, shelled
¾ cup sugar
1 tsp grated zest of an
  organic orange
salt
pomegranate seeds

Garnishes
pistachios, almonds, shredded
coconut, ground cinnamon

Our friend Elif got the recipe for this Turkish classic from her mother-in-law and refined it with chestnuts and orange zest. When she sent us the recipe, as we had asked, we couldn't believe our eyes: it served 50 people! She recommended a 3-quart pot for 6 pounds of sugar! Elif explained that in Turkey, aşure is always a shared dish and the more you make, the better, because family, friends, and neighbors will expect some. This seemed a great idea to us, but we still reduced the quantity to suit eight people.

Put the spelt, chickpeas, and beans in a pot, cover with plenty of water and soak overnight.

The next day dice the dried figs and apricots and put in a small pot, together with the raisins, cinnamon stick, and cloves. Add the milk and heat over low heat until warm. Remove from the heat and let the dried fruits and spices soak for 30 minutes.

Drain the soaking water from the wheat, chickpeas, and beans and add about 2½ cups of water to the pot. Bring to a boil, reduce the heat, and simmer for about 30 minutes. Remove from the heat and set aside.

Remove the cinnamon stick and cloves from the dried fruit and milk mixture and add the mixture to the wheat, chickpeas, and beans in the pot. Peel the pear and apple, dice both and add to the pot and stir. Add the walnuts, chestnuts, sugar, orange zest, and a pinch of salt and simmer over low heat for 1 hour, stirring occasionally and adding a little bit of warm water as needed so that the pudding doesn't stick to the pot.

To serve, give the pudding one more good stir, then spoon into small bowls. Scatter plenty of pomegranate seeds on top, which give the pudding a delicious freshness. Serve decorated with pistachios, almonds, shredded coconut, and ground cinnamon.

kaymaklı kayısı tatlısı

Cinnamon Apricots with Cream

serves 4

gluten-free

Time
about 35 minutes

Ingredients
⅔ cup dried apricots
¾ cup orange juice
1 Tbsp sugar
½ tsp ground cinnamon
½ cup walnuts, chopped
¾ cup clotted cream

Goes well with
Turkish coffee and baklava

Malatya, a town in eastern Anatolia, is an apricot-lover's mecca, for it's the home of the aromatic fruit. Apricots taste best when eaten fresh, but they're also delicious dried, especially with cinnamon and clotted cream.

Put the apricots, orange juice, sugar, and cinnamon in a small pot and bring to a boil. Reduce the heat and simmer for 15 minutes. Remove the apricots from the pot and set aside. Reduce the liquid to a syrup over medium heat, stirring occasionally, until you have about 3 tablespoons of syrup, about 10 minutes. Remove from the heat and let cool.

Toast the chopped walnuts in a frying pan over medium heat for about 4 minutes, stirring occasionally so that they don't burn. Remove the nuts from the pan and let cool.

Arrange the apricots on four small plates, add a dollop of clotted cream to each plate, drizzle with the syrup, and sprinkle with walnuts.

cezerye

Carrot Ginger Squares

makes about 30

vegan + gluten-free

Time
about 1 hour
(+ 45 minutes for cooking)

Ingredients
3 large carrots
1 cup sugar
pinch cinnamon
pinch ground cloves
pinch ground ginger
2 tsp lemon juice
3 Tbsp chopped pistachios
  or walnuts
5 Tbsp shredded coconut

Goes well with
a cup of tea

Tip
Cezerye keeps well. Store
the squares in an airtight
container at room temperature
and they'll keep for 10 days.

Oddly enough, *havuçlu kek*, carrot cake, is served in almost all of Istanbul's cafes. The Turks like their carrots served sweet, just like in *cezerye*, a kind of carrot candy. No one who tries this for the first time can believe it—is this really carrot? Yum, so delicious!

Peel and grate the carrots. In a medium pot bring ½ cup water to a boil and add the grated carrots. Cover the pot and cook over medium heat for 20 minutes. After 15 minutes, see if the carrots are sticking to the bottom of the pot; if they are, add a little hot water.

Add the sugar, cinnamon, cloves, ginger, and lemon juice. Simmer the mixture, uncovered, over low heat until all the liquid has evaporated, stirring occasionally. After about 45 minutes you should have a sticky paste that smells slightly of caramel. Add the chopped pistachios, stir vigorously with a pastry scraper, then spread the paste onto a baking sheet lined with parchment paper and let cool.

Transfer the carrot paste, with the parchment paper still attached, to a large cutting board and cut the paste into small squares. Sprinkle both sides of the carrot squares with shredded coconut.

If they are too soft, let the squares air-dry for an hour or two; they'll get firmer. If you like, instead of cutting the paste into squares, you can roll it into small balls.

Evening

[akşam]

Lion's milk and other delicious things

For *akşam yemeği*, the evening meal, people in Istanbul gather around mother's table (mother is *anne* in Turkish), at a *meyhane* (tavern or bar), or at a friend's *(arkadas)* house.

Whichever it is, the most important meal of the day begins with meze, a variety of foods served in small bowls and dishes that quickly transform the table to a bright festive scene. Bowls of carrots and zucchini swim in yogurt sauce next to bowls of sweet marinated vegetables and fresh salads with tomato, parsley, mint, and lots of onions.

You eat quietly, meaning with plenty of time, because quiet it isn't: a heated discussion about the latest soccer game dominates the evening, mixed with telephone conversations with friends, all while the TV runs in the background.

When the food tastes especially good, it will be praised and the hands of the cook will be wished good health—*eline sağlik*—thus expressing one's delight about the delicious meal.

fava

White Bean Purée with Lemon & Dill

serves 4

vegan + gluten-free

Time
about 15 minutes

Ingredients
1 onion
2 Tbsp sunflower oil
½ can white beans
juice of ½ lemon
1 bunch of dill, roughly
  chopped
⅔ cup olive oil
salt
pepper

Doesn't *fava* sound smooth? And that is exactly what it is, sooo creamy! Isabel loves this starter. At her home it's often on the table, simply because it's easy to prepare and tastes delicious any time of the year. When Isa goes out to eat in Istanbul and wants some good *fava*, she makes her way to Karaköy Lokantası in the district of the same name.

Peel and dice the onion. Heat the sunflower oil in a pan and sauté the onion until transparent.

Drain the beans well. Put in a large bowl and add the remaining ingredients. Using a handheld electric mixer, blend the ingredients finely.

If you like, serve the purée as a firm cube (this is the traditional way): cover the inside of a square airtight container with plastic wrap, fill with the purée, smooth it down to fill all the corners of the container, and place in the fridge overnight. The next day turn out the *fava* onto a plate.

From great love
to little meals

... and with the right drink, too!

Turkish appetizers, meze, and traditional aniseed liquor are an inseparable pair, making for long, satisfying evenings of food and conversation in a traditional Turkish bar (meyhane).

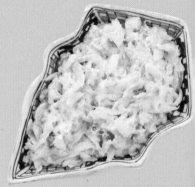

The classic start to meze is *beyaz peynir*, sheep's cheese with honeydew melon. The simple sweet-savory combination is brought to your table without being ordered and is the starting point for the whole cold meze, or *zeytinyağli mezeler*. Then the waiter arrives with a huge tray filled with small dishes. The guests gaze at this colorful mosaic for a moment, ask some questions, such as which dishes are vegetarian (*Bu vejetaryen mı?*), then pick out some favorites. These appear immediately, set out in the middle of the table for all to share, served with a fresh loaf of white bread and, of course, *rakı*.

The unofficial national drink* is served in a glass filled to two or three fingers. Then water is added, then ice cubes, in that order. The liquor turns a creamy white color that is known as "lion's milk" (*aslan sütü*), as *rakı* is referred to with a knowing wink. Glasses are raised with *şerefe*, a toast to honor.

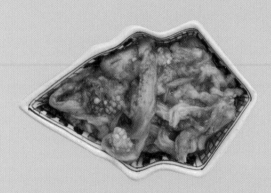

Water and raki

Once the cold appetizers are finished, the meal continues with warm meze like *sigara böreği* (pastry rolls filled with cheese) or *içli köfte* (stuffed bulgur pastries). These are served with even more *rakı* and water. Anyone who wants to continue on orders a meat main course like *hünkar beğendi* (lamb stew). Or everyone might share a grilled *çipura* (dorade) or deep-fried *hamsi* (anchovies).

A Turkish dinner always closes with tea and a plate of fresh fruit: apples and oranges in winter, watermelon and peaches in summer. This makes for a perfect end to an evening of *rakı*.

*The official national drink is the alcohol-free yogurt drink *ayran*.

---

havuç salatası / Carrot Yogurt

serves 4

vegetarian
 + gluten-free

Time
about 15 minutes

Ingredients
2 Tbsp walnuts, chopped
2 large carrots
2 Tbsp olive oil
1 garlic clove
1¾ cups plain
 whole-milk yogurt
1 tsp lemon juice
¼ tsp red pepper flakes
1 tsp tahini (optional)
salt
pepper

Toast the chopped walnuts in a frying pan over medium heat for about 4 minutes, stirring occasionally and making sure they don't burn. Pour the nuts into a bowl and let cool. Peel the carrots and grate roughly. Heat the oil in another pan. Peel and crush the garlic clove, add to the pan with the grated carrots, and sauté for about 5 minutes. Remove from the heat and let cool. In a bowl, combine the yogurt with the walnuts, garlicky carrots, lemon juice, and pepper flakes. Stir in the tahini, if using. Season with salt and plenty of pepper.

yogurtlu kabak ezme

Zucchini Yogurt with Hazelnuts

serves 4

vegetarian + gluten-free

Time
about 15 minutes
(+ 15 minutes for resting)

Ingredients
2 Tbsp hazelnuts, chopped
2 large zucchini
2-3 Tbsp olive oil
1 garlic clove
1¾ cups plain whole-milk
  yogurt
¼ tsp dried mint
1 tsp lemon juice
salt
pepper

Goes well with
fresh loaf of white bread and
preferably even more meze

This classic meze with zucchini is the perfect between-meals snack. Spread it on whole-wheat bread—it makes a delicious vegetarian sandwich.

Toast the hazelnuts in a frying pan over medium heat for about 4 minutes, stirring occasionally and making sure they don't burn. Pour the nuts into a bowl and let cool.

Using the large holes of a grater, shred the zucchini roughly. Place in a colander set over a bowl, sprinkle with salt, and let drain for about 15 minutes. Squeeze out any liquid, using the back of the tablespoon and pressing the shredded zucchini against the colander.

Heat some olive oil in another pan. Peel and crush the garlic clove, add to the pan with the shredded zucchini, and sauté for about 5 minutes. Remove from the heat and let cool.

In a bowl, combine the yogurt, hazelnuts, garlicky zucchini, dried mint, and lemon juice. Season with salt and plenty of pepper.

çerkez tavuğu

Yogurt with Chicken and Walnuts

serves 4

gluten-free

Time
about 15 minutes
(+ 30 minutes for cooking)

Ingredients
2 chicken breasts
a few soup vegetables
   (such as leeks and
   carrots; optional)
bay leaf (optional)
4 Tbsp walnuts, chopped
1¾ cups plain whole-milk
   yogurt
4 Tbsp cornichon liquid
1 garlic clove
pinch of ground cumin
salt
pepper
6 small cornichons, finely
   chopped
1 tsp lemon juice

Think yogurt with chicken is unusual? Well, it's unusually delicious! It takes quite some preparation, as the chicken has to be shredded extremely thin for this dish to reach its best consistency, but the time spent is well worth it.

Bring a large pot of salted water to a boil. Add the chicken breasts and simmer over low heat for 30 minutes. Add the soup vegetables and bay leaf, if using, to the chicken. (That way, you've got the basis for a homemade noodle soup for the next day.)

Toast the walnuts in a frying pan over medium heat for about 4 minutes, stirring occasionally and making sure they don't burn. Pour the nuts into a bowl and let cool.

Put the yogurt in a bowl and stir in the cornichon liquid. Peel and crush the garlic clove and add it to the yogurt. Season with a pinch of cumin, salt, and plenty of pepper. Add the walnuts and cornichons.

Shred the chicken breasts finely. Add the chicken and lemon juice to the bowl and stir well.

A quick TEA on the ferry before DINNER!

acılı ezme

Tomato Salad with Dill & Mint

serves 4

vegan + gluten-free

Time
about 20 minutes
(+ 15 minutes for marinating)

Ingredients
4 large tomatoes
5 sprigs dill
4 sprigs mint
½ bunch parsley
3 green onions
1 tsp green chile, finely
  chopped (optional)
2 Tbsp olive oil
1 tsp red pepper flakes
salt
pepper

This herby tomato salad has a light zing to it thanks to green onions and a sprinkling of red pepper flakes. It beautifully complements a mild yogurt-based starter. If you're like Veronika and like the salad hotter, serve it with chopped chile.

Bring a large pot of water to a boil and remove from the heat. Using a sharp knife, cut a shallow X in the bottom of the tomatoes and place the tomatoes in the hot water. After about 2–3 minutes remove the tomatoes with a slotted spoon and let cool on a plate. Peel the skin off with a knife.

Dice the tomatoes finely and put in a bowl. Rinse and dry the herbs, chop finely, and add to the bowl with the tomatoes. Rinse the green onions, cut into thin rings, and add to the bowl. Add the chile, if using.

Drizzle the salad with the oil and add the pepper flakes. Season with salt and pepper. Stir well and let rest for 15 minutes before serving.

patlican ezmesi

Roasted Eggplant & Garlic Purée

serves 4

vegetarian + gluten-free

Time
about 15 minutes
(+ 45 minutes for baking)

Ingredients
4 large eggplants
2 garlic cloves
¼ cup soft butter
salt
pepper
plain whole-milk yogurt
  (optional)
1 Tbsp tahini (optional)
1 Tbsp chopped fresh parsley

Goes well with
fresh loaf of white bread
and meze

This eggplant purée is a true meze classic, even though it might not be the most visually appealing. It tastes so delicious that you will quickly overlook its appearance. We think this brownish dip is quite wonderful!

If you're barbecuing, you can prepare the purée easily: just put the eggplants on the grill; they will cook much quicker than in an oven and acquire a wonderful smoky taste.

Preheat the oven to 375°F.

With a fork, prick the eggplants several times all over so that they don't explode in the oven and place them on a baking sheet lined with parchment paper. Roast on the top rack of the oven for 45 minutes. (If your oven has a grill, you can use it instead, if you like.) Remove the eggplants and let cool slightly.

Cut the eggplants in half lengthwise. Scoop out the flesh with a spoon and put it into a bowl. Peel and crush the garlic cloves and add them to the bowl with the eggplant. Stir in the butter. Season with salt and pepper.

If you'd like the purée to be more creamy or nutty, add the yogurt or the tahini. Sprinkle with parsley and serve.

Senem Ekin Sen

Senem, who was born in Turkey, likes Toronto, eggplant, and dogs. Apart from these, the yoga teacher with Canadian roots has a weakness for *patlıcan ezmesi* (see recipe, page 108) and *cacık* (recipe below). Neither of these mezes contains nuts, to which she is allergic. In Istanbul, she enjoys the things she missed the most: endless meze evenings at big, fully loaded tables with loud conversations and even louder laughter. You can often find her on the Asian side of the city in the *meyhane* Deniz Yıldızı in Kadıköy. When Senem visits Avrupa Yakası (the European side), she goes to the restaurant Naif in the old harbor district Karaköy.

cacık / Yogurt with Cucumber & Mint

serves 4

vegetarian + gluten-free

Time
about 15 minutes

Ingredients
3 small cucumbers
salt
1¾ cups plain whole-milk
  yogurt
1 garlic clove
1 tsp lemon juice
5 sprigs dill, chopped
¼ tsp dried mint
olive oil
pepper

Peel the cucumbers and cut in half lengthwise. Scrape out the seeds with a spoon. Grate the cucumber halves finely. Place in a colander set over a bowl and sprinkle with ½ teaspoon salt and let stand for about 10 minutes. Squeeze out any liquid, pressing the grated cucumbers against the colander with a spoon.

Put the yogurt in a bowl. Peel and crush the garlic cloves and add them to the bowl with the yogurt and stir together. Add the lemon juice, dill, mint, and oil. Season with salt and pepper.

Purslane

Semizotu—purslane—is available in summer. In Turkey, come March, everyone is simmering with excitement in anticipation of purslane's arrival in the markets.

This wild plant also grows farther north, but in modern times has been mostly forgotten. In the old days it was known as verdolaga, pigweed, hogweed, and red root.

Purslane's fleshy leaves are reminiscent of lamb's lettuce, and the taste of its stems is similar to cucumber.

Purslane is actually an aggressively spreading weed (each plant produces more than 50,000 new seeds) that has brought many gardeners to their wit's end.

Rich in vitamin C and omega-3 oils, this green summer plant is not only tasty but extremely healthy. It's delicious in smoothies.

semizotu salatası
Purslane Salad with Mint & Figs

serves 4

vegan + gluten-free

Time about 15 minutes

Ingredients
1 lb purslane
½ bunch mint
3 green onions
½ can chickpeas, drained
4 figs
goat cheese, sliced (optional)
4 Tbsp walnuts, chopped

For the dressing
6 Tbsp olive oil
3 Tbsp lemon juice
2 Tbsp tahini
1 Tbsp honey
2 Tbsp orange juice

Goes well with
açma (see recipe, page 29)

Tip
Use melon or blueberries
instead of figs.

Purslane makes a fine pesto or soup, but we like it best in a salad, and particularly in this fresh and fruity version with mint and figs.

Wash the purslane and remove the lower broad stalks. Tear into bite-size pieces and put in a large bowl. Rinse and dry the mint and pinch off the leaves. Rinse the green onions and cut into narrow rings. Add the mint leaves, green onions, and chickpeas to the bowl. Cut the figs into quarters (you can peel them if you like) and add them to the bowl. Add the goat cheese, if using.

Toast the walnuts in a pan over medium heat for about 4 minutes, stirring occasionally and making sure they don't burn. Remove the nuts from the pan and let cool.

Put the ingredients for the dressing into a small bowl, whisk well, and season with salt and pepper. Pour over the salad, add the walnuts, and toss well.

'taze balık'
means fresh Fish!

With its proximity to the sea,
Istanbul brims with fish markets.

balık

[fresh fish]

1. *barbun/* <u>red mullet</u>

2. *istavrit/*<u>mackerel</u>

3. *sardalya/*<u>sardine</u>

4. *hamsi/*<u>anchovy</u>

5. *mezgit/*<u>whiting</u>

6. *karides/* <u>prawn</u>

7. *kalamar/*<u>squid</u>

8. *kalkan/*<u>turbot</u>

12. *dil balığı/*
sole

11. *levrek/*
European sea bass

9. *lüfer/*
snapper

10. *palamut/bonito*

13. *çipura/porgy*

14. *mercan/red porgy*

hamsi yaprak sarması

Anchovies in Vine Leaves with Sea Beans

serves 4

Time
about 70 minutes

Ingredients
1 lb anchovies
  (gutted, if you like)
3 Tbsp olive oil
juice of ½ lemon
pepper
1 jar pickled vine leaves
1¼ lb sea beans
2 Tbsp butter
¼ cup orzo
1 cup rice
salt
2 lemons

Goes well with
The traditional side
dish with fish is *roka*
(large-leaved arugula,
see page 31), without
a dressing.

The typical *meyhane* (a bar that serves fish and *rakı*) doesn't make much fuss about fish preparation: it's either grilled or fried. Period. The Turkish *meyhane* cook would never have the idea of rolling small Black Sea anchovies in vine leaves. That would take a couple of crazy *yabancılar* foreigners like us...

Rinse the anchovies and place in a large bowl. Pour over the oil and lemon juice, season with pepper and marinate for 10 minutes. Preheat the oven to 400°F (if your oven has a grill, use that). Take half the vine leaves from the package and rinse thoroughly under running cold water. (Use the rest of the vine leaves for another dish.) Let dry briefly on a clean kitchen towel. Using scissors, cut the vine leaves in half. Wrap an anchovy in half a vine leaf; it's fine for the head and tail to show.

Place the wrapped anchovies next to each other onto a baking sheet lined with parchment paper and roast on the top rack (or under the grill) for 10 minutes.

In the meantime, put the sea beans in a colander and wash well. Bring a large pot of water to a boil, add the sea beans, and cook for 10 minutes. Drain and rinse quickly with cold water. Remove the tender green stems from the stringy central core by holding onto the core and gently pulling off the stems.

Heat the butter in a large pan and add the orzo. Fry until the orzo is lightly golden. Add the rice, salt, and water and cook until the rice is done according to the directions on package.

Serve the anchovies with the sea beans, the pasta and rice mix, and fresh lemon wedges.

hünkar beğendi

Lamb Stew with Eggplant Béchamel

serves 4

Time
about 40 minutes
(+ 2½ hours for cooking)

Ingredients
6 eggplants
1 large onion
2 green bell peppers
1⅓ lb lamb, diced
4 Tbsp sunflower oil
2 garlic cloves
1 can (14 oz) whole peeled
  tomatoes, drained
2 Tbsp paprika paste
1 tsp honey
salt
pepper
red pepper flakes
½ cup butter
3 Tbsp flour
1½ cups milk
2 Tbsp Gouda cheese, grated
ground nutmeg

Goes well with
rice

This dish is so wonderfully creamy and soft that you feel you could bathe in it. The sultan also enjoyed it: translated, *hünkar beğendi* means "the ruler is delighted." We are, too!

Preheat the oven to 375°F. (If your oven has a grill, use that.)

Using a fork, prick the eggplants all over so that they don't explode in the oven and place on a baking sheet lined with parchment paper. Roast the eggplants on the top rack for about 45 minutes. Remove from the oven and let cool.

Dice the onion and pepper finely and set aside. Heat the sunflower oil in a large pot and brown the lamb quickly on all sides. Add the onion and peppers. Peel and crush the garlic cloves and add to the pot. Stir well and sauté for a few minutes.

Chop the tomatoes roughly and add to the pot together with the paprika paste and honey. Add water so that the meat is completely covered.

Simmer, uncovered, over low heat for at least 2½ hours until the meat is soft and almost falls apart. Season with salt, pepper, and pepper flakes.

For the eggplant béchamel, cut the cooled eggplants in half lengthwise and, using a spoon, scrape the flesh into a bowl.

Melt the butter in a pan, add the flour, and let sweat over low heat for about 2 minutes, stirring constantly so that the flour doesn't burn. Slowly add the milk and continue to stir. Add the eggplant flesh, followed by the Gouda.

Season the eggplant béchamel with salt and nutmeg. Arrange the béchamel on plates and ladle the lamb stew in the middle.

Veronika's
favorite dish

A view of Istanbul's Galata Bridge

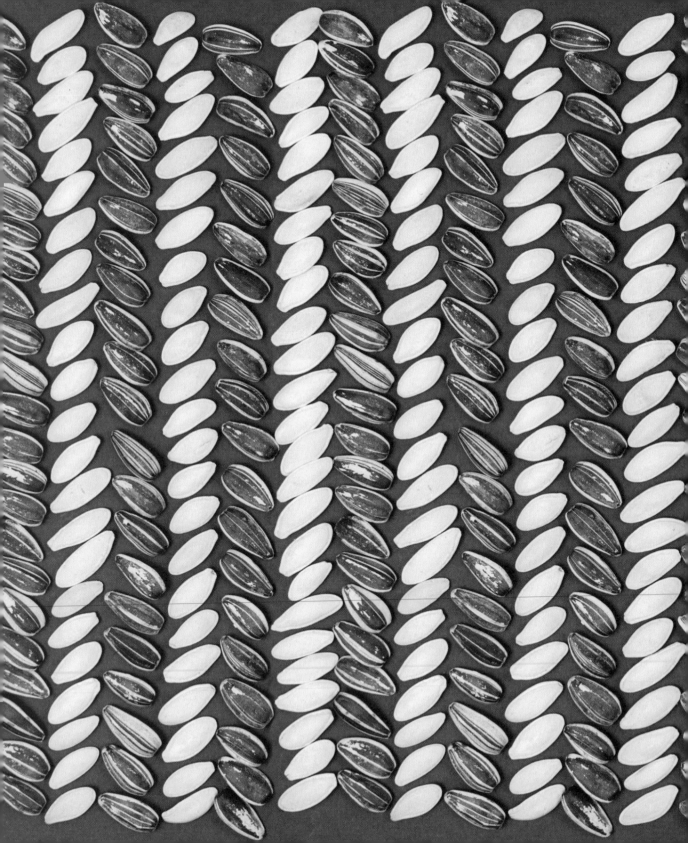

NIGHT

[gece]

super snacks

Istanbul doesn't sleep. Ever. And so there's always somewhere and something to eat. The city offers a huge range of snacks and sumptuous meals for busy nightshift workers and partying clubbers.

Istanbul may rob you of your sleep, but you won't be hungry while it's happening. In the early hours, just follow your nose through the alleyways until you find a place on a street corner selling *pide* (stuffed flatbreads) or *lahmacun* (Turkish pizza)—that way, you can experience culinary delights long after dancing!

Iyi geceler, goodnight! Or even better: *günaydın*, good morning!

cevizli lahmacun

Turkish Nut Pizza

makes 4 pizzas

vegetarian

Time
about 1 hour
(+ 45 minutes for resting
and 10 minutes for baking)

Ingredients
For the dough
1 package active dry yeast
½ cup milk
2¾ cup whole-wheat flour
1 tsp salt

For the topping
2 garlic cloves
1 onion
1 yellow bell pepper
1 large tomato
¾ cup walnuts
2 Tbsp paprika paste
1 tsp tomato paste
1 Tbsp olive oil
1 tsp red pepper flakes
½ tsp cumin
½ tsp sumac
salt
pepper
½ cup flat-leaf parsley,
  leaves, for garnish
1 lemon, quartered

Goes well with
ayran (yogurt drink)

When it comes to *lahmacun*, "Turkish pizza" topped with ground meat, Lisa, a vegetarian, occasionally makes an exception—it's that good. Here, we've created a vegetarian version with plenty of walnuts, and we like it better than the versions with meat. If you prefer the classic version with ground meat, use 8 ounces ground beef or lamb instead of the nuts.

For the dough, combine 4¼ cups water, the yeast, and milk in a small bowl. Let rest briefly. Put the flour and salt in a large bowl and add the yeast and milk mixture. Knead with your hands until you get a smooth dough. Let the dough rest for 45 minutes.

For the topping, peel the garlic cloves and onion and chop finely. Dice the pepper and tomato finely. Chop the walnuts finely. Put the garlic, onion, pepper, tomato, and walnuts in a large bowl and add the paprika paste, tomato paste, oil, pepper flakes, cumin, and sumac. Season the mixture with salt and pepper.

Set oven racks in the upper and lower third of the oven and preheat the oven and two baking sheets to 450°F.

Put a moist kitchen towel on a work surface and a piece of parchment paper the size of your baking sheets on the towel (that way, the parchment paper will stay in place). Roll out the dough to two thin (¼-inch) rectangular or oval shapes (about 12 by 6 inches). Spread half the filling on each piece of dough all the way to the edge of the dough.

Take the two baking sheets out of the oven and place one *lahmacun*, with the parchment paper, on each. Return them to the oven and bake for about 10 minutes. Halfway through the baking time, switch the baking sheets between the racks so that the pizzas cook evenly.

Sprinkle with parsley leaves and serve with lemon wedges for squeezing over.

Stuffed Turkish Flatbread

makes 4 pastry boats

Time
about 50 minutes
(+ 45 minutes for resting)

Ingredients
For the dough
4¼ cups flour
1 tsp salt
¾ cup milk
1 tsp sugar
1 cube fresh active yeast
5 Tbsp olive oil

For the sausage topping
2 oz garlic sausage, sliced
2 eggs
1 tsp red pepper flakes

For the spinach topping
1 cup spinach, chopped
¼ cup feta cheese, crumbled
1 Tbsp raisins
1 small onion, chopped

For both toppings
salt
pepper
olive oil
1 egg yolk, beaten
1 Tbsp black cumin seeds

Tip
Feta, figs, and walnuts make another delicious topping.

When ordering *pide*, Turkey's slightly chewy flatbread, in Istanbul, you will likely be asked if you want it with *yumurta* (egg). We think egg goes fabulously well with *sucuk*, Turkish garlic sausage, and decided to include it in this recipe for an open-faced *pide*. But we're also great fans of vegetarian *pide*, like the slightly unusual variation with spinach, onions, and raisins.

Combine the flour and salt in a large bowl. Put the milk, ¾ cup water and the sugar in a small pot, heat over heat until tepid, and stir in the yeast. Once the sugar and yeast have dissolved, set the pot aside and let cool. Add the oil to the flour in the bowl and knead with your hands until you get a smooth dough. Cover the bowl with a clean kitchen towel and let the dough rest in a warm place for 45 minutes.

Knead the dough on a work surface sprinkled with flour. Break off 1 quarter of the dough and roll out to a flat oval (about 12 by 6 inches) about ½ inch thick. For the sausage topping, cover the dough with sausage, leaving a 1-inch border. Season with salt and pepper and drizzle with oil. Fold up the long sides of the oval so that the topping is partly covered and enclosed.

Place the *pide* on a baking sheet lined with parchment paper. Crack an egg into the middle and sprinkle with some pepper flakes. Repeat the process with another quarter of dough.

Preheat the oven to 475°F.

Use the remaining dough to make the two vegetarian *pide*. Scatter some spinach on the dough and add the feta cheese, raisins, and onion. Season with salt and pepper and drizzle with oil. Fold up the long sides of the ovals so that the topping is partly covered and enclosed and pinch the ends together. Place the vegetarian *pide* next to the *pide* with sausage on the baking sheet.

Brush the edges of all three *pide* with the beaten egg yolk and sprinkle with black cumin seeds. Bake in the preheated oven on the middle rack for 15–17 minutes.

Dates and the Sugar Feast, or Şeker Bayramı

Food in times of fasting

Muslims in Turkey observe *ramazam*, a four-week-long annual fasting period. The dates of *ramazam* change from year to year, because they are calculated on the Islamic lunar calendar. What doesn't change is that eating and drinking only take place between sunset and dawn.

When the sun is down, the muezzins call for the evening breaking of the fast. This often takes place in large groups, as hospitality is particularly valued at these times. In the shopping area of Istiklal Caddesi in Beyoğlu, believers will spread an extra-large tablecloth on the ground, sit down, and share their delicacies with everyone present.

Traditionally, those who fast will eat dried dates with water directly after sundown. The dried fruit is a powerful source of glucose and soon gives strength to those weak from fasting. Soup is served next, before substantial starters and main courses.

Breaking the fast with dates and water

Cooking is lavish during *ramazam*, with all kinds of meze and sumptuous, hearty meat dishes being prepared. These are served with water and *ayran* (a yogurt drink), because alcohol is forbidden during fasting. The long evening is rounded off with a variety of sweets.

Those not fasting can also join in. Many restaurants have special *ramazam* menus; it's a wonderful moment when everyone begins to eat together as the muezzin calls.

When the four-week fasting period ends, Muslims reward themselves with the long-anticipated Sugar Feast (*şeker bayrami*), a sweet finale to the fast. The feast lasts for three days, during which families eat richly and consume many confections. Sweets such as *lokum*, baklava, and bonbons are given as gifts, the kids get some cash, and everyone is delighted to have survived the fast. Friends, family, and even some tourists wish each other *"Iyi bayramlar!"*—happy holiday!

Breaking the fast at sundown in the park

irmik helvası
Pudding with Cinnamon & Pine Nuts

serves 4

Time
about 20 minutes

Ingredients
1¼ cups milk
⅓ cup sugar
¼ cup butter
½ cup semolina
½ cup pine nuts
dried fruit, such as apricots
   or raisins (optional)
1 tsp ground cinnamon

Goes well with
yogurt ice cream or
clotted cream

Isabel loves this simple dessert. When she wants a late snack and there's no pistachio chocolate (see page 58) in the house, she picks up her trusty wooden spoon and makes a portion of *irmik helvası*. If her husband is in luck, he'll get some, too!

Bring the milk and sugar to a boil in a pot, stirring occasionally until the sugar is dissolved. Remove from the heat and set aside.

Melt the butter in a large pan and add the semolina. Cook over medium heat, stirring constantly. Add the pine nuts after about 5 minutes and continue to cook for another 15 minutes, stirring constantly.

Slowly add the milk and sugar mixture (be careful, it splatters) and continue to stir until the consistency becomes slightly grainy.

Add the dried fruit, if using. Remove from the heat, stir in the cinnamon, and divide among four small plates to serve.

Isabel's favorite sweet

Eggplant

Eggplant is sometimes referred to as aubergine, which is its British and French name. Eggplant originated in Asia, but is featured in cuisines worldwide.

Be sure to cook eggplant, because raw eggplant contains a poison, solanine, that will give you a bad stomachache. Cooking eggplant eliminates this problem.

In Turkish cuisine, eggplant is usually accompanied by garlic, tomatoes, ground meat, and yogurt.

The best-known variety of eggplant is 'Black King', which is dark violet in color, but there are other varieties with lighter tints, such as pink, as found in graffiti eggplants, to white.

When it comes to cooking oil, the eggplant is a real sponge. When frying, it will suck up the oil in seconds. Pre-salting or soaking the eggplant in saltwater will help prevent this, remove the bitter taste, and leave some oil in the pan.

Turks love eggplants and have since the Ottoman era. They have more than two hundred different eggplant recipes!

imam bayıldı

Stuffed Eggplant

serves 4

vegan + gluten-free

Time
about 25 minutes

Ingredients
4 large eggplants
salt

4 large tomatoes
2 onions
2 garlic cloves
3 red bell peppers
about 6 Tbsp olive oil
pinch sugar
1 tsp red pepper flakes
2 tsp fresh thyme leaves,
    chopped
pepper

The name of this dish translates as "the imam swooned." The story behind the name is unknown, but many think it earned its moniker because he ate so much of this wonderful food. Others say it was because of the amount of costly olive oil used in its preparation. Either way, we remain fully conscious when we fill the purple fruits.

Peel the eggplants lengthwise in such a way that you create a pattern of alternating strips of peel and flesh. Cut the eggplants across in the middle, sprinkle with salt, let rest for 10 minutes, then dab dry with a paper towel. Remove some flesh with a tablespoon, chop finely, and set aside. Bring a large pot of water to a boil and remove from the heat. Using a sharp knife, cut a shallow X in the bottom of the tomatoes and place the tomatoes in the hot water. After about 2–3 minutes remove the tomatoes with a slotted spoon and let cool on a plate. Peel the skin off with a knife and dice the tomatoes finely.

Peel the onions and garlic cloves and chop finely. Dice the peppers finely. Heat 3 tablespoons oil in a pan and sauté the onions and garlic until transparent. Add the peppers, chopped eggplant, and tomatoes. Stir and simmer for a few minutes. Remove the pan from the heat and add a pinch of sugar, the pepper flakes, and thyme to the sauce. Season with salt and pepper. Preheat the oven to 350°F.

Heat the remaining oil in a second pan and sauté the eggplants on both sides. Place on a baking sheet lined with parchment paper, carefully fill with the sauce, and drizzle with oil. Bake the eggplants in the oven for about 30–40 minutes.

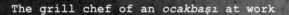

The grill chef of an *ocakbaşı* at work

dürüm

Spiced Lamb & Pistachio Wraps

serves 4

Time
about 30 minutes

Ingredients
1¼ cups plain whole-milk
  yogurt
salt
2 garlic cloves
1 large onion
1 cup pistachios
1 lb ground lamb
1 tbsp paprika paste
1 egg
1 tsp red pepper flakes
1 tsp sumac
½ tsp ground cumin
pinch ground cinnamon
½ tsp salt
½ tsp pepper
olive oil

Accompaniments
flatbread, parsley, mint,
sliced onions, and tomatoes

Goes well with
şalgam, a savory vegetable
juice (usually made from
radish, beetroot, and carrots)

To grill the meat for a wrap (dürüm), Turks use traditional skewers that are broader and flatter than conventional skewers, because they hold the ground meat best (see photo, page 141). For the best results, use the flattest skewers you can find. A fiery version of this recipe is the adana kebab; you omit the nuts and use three times as much red pepper flakes. Don't use the mild sweet variety but acı, the hot one.

Put the yogurt in a small bowl and add a bit of salt. Peel and crush one of the garlic cloves and add it to the yogurt. Set the bowl aside.

Peel the onion, chop finely, and put in a large bowl. Peel and crush the other garlic clove and add it to the bowl. Chop the pistachios roughly. (This works best if you put the pistachios in a plastic freezer bag and pound them with a small pot.) Add the pistachios to the bowl with the onion and garlic, followed by the ground lamb, paprika paste, egg, pepper flakes, sumac, cumin, and cinnamon.

Using your hands, combine the lamb with all the ingredients. Take one quarter of the mixture and shape it around a skewer to an even, flat sausage shape about 8 inches long. If the mixture becomes too sticky, rinse your hands with water while shaping the mixture. Brush the meat with oil on both sides. Repeat with the remaining meat mixture until you have four flat sausage shapes. Brush all sides of the skewered meat with a bit of oil.

Place the four skewers on a hot grill and grill for about 3 minutes on each side. Warm up the flatbread on the grill as well.

Serve the kebabs, flatbread, garlicky yogurt, and other accompaniments in individual bowls or on plates so that everyone can make their own dürüm.

et yemeKleri

[savory bites]

Whether it's chicken, lamb, or beef, kebabs *(şiş)* are dearly beloved in Istanbul (see recipe, page 142).

Döner simply means "to turn," and *kebab* is the word for "grilled meat." When you order a *döner kebab*, you get a portion of well-seasoned lamb (or beef) slices from the rotating spit with some accompaniments. If you prefer your *kebab* in some bread, order a *pide döner*. Traditionally, *kebabs* are not served with sauce.

Köfte, the mini burgers with extra-fine bulgur in the mix, are usually served with rice and salad.

Liver *(ciğer)* is the most popular offal from the grill and is often eaten in a *dürüm*.

A special preparation for a beef burger *(islak)* is to cover the bun in a tomato and garlic sauce. It's a messy but delicious treat, especially at five in the morning!

Dürüm means roll or wrap. The meat from the grill is rolled in flatbread with salad and onions.

Toasted bread with garlic sausage and cheese *(karaşik tost)* is served at every stall and on ferries. Vegetarians order *kasarlı tost* (with cheese only).

Çig köfte are longish meatballs made from raw ground lamb. While the sale of raw meat in the streets is forbidden, the vegan version with bulgur and seasoning is usually available.

Lahmacun is a paper-thin, crispy flatbread spread with a deliciously spicy sauce made from ground meat, bell peppers, and tomatoes. The perfect topping: parsley and a bit of lemon juice (see recipe, page 128).

Iskender kebab is a dish of layers: toasted flatbread layered with tomato sauce, then yogurt, and finally with lamb. The whole thing is served with a large portion of melted butter. A delicious calorie bomb!

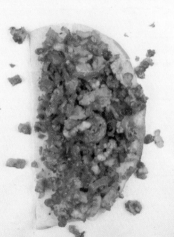

Kokoreç are lamb intestines grilled over charcoal. They are served finely chopped with onions and tomatoes in bread.

'Islak' burgers look a bit strange but make an excellent midnight snack!

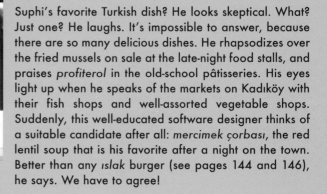

Suphi Yilmaz

Suphi's favorite Turkish dish? He looks skeptical. What? Just one? He laughs. It's impossible to answer, because there are so many delicious dishes. He rhapsodizes over the fried mussels on sale at the late-night food stalls, and praises *profiterol* in the old-school pâtisseries. His eyes light up when he speaks of the markets on Kadıköy with their fish shops and well-assorted vegetable shops. Suddenly, this well-educated software designer thinks of a suitable candidate after all: *mercimek çorbası*, the red lentil soup that is his favorite after a night on the town. Better than any *ıslak* burger (see pages 144 and 146), he says. We have to agree!

mercimek çorbası / Lentil Soup

serves 4

vegan + gluten-free

Time
about 15 minutes
(+ 30 minutes
   for cooking)

Ingredients
1 large onion
1 large carrot
3 Tbsp sunflower oil
1 cup red lentils

about 2½ cups
   vegetable stock
1 Tbsp paprika paste
2 tsp red pepper
   flakes
1 tsp sumac
½ tsp ground cumin
salt
pepper
3-4 sprigs parsley,
   chopped
3-4 sprigs mint,
   chopped
1 lemon, quartered

Peel the onion and carrot and dice finely. Heat the sunflower oil in a large pot, add the onion and carrot and sauté over medium heat for about 2 minutes, stirring. Add the lentils and cook for 2 minutes longer. Add the vegetable stock and bring to a boil. Reduce the heat and simmer for about 30 minutes. Add some hot water or more stock if the soup seems too thick.

Add the paprika paste, pepper flakes, sumac, and cumin and season the soup with salt and pepper. If you prefer a creamier soup, purée the soup with a handheld mixer. It's equally delicious chunky, though! Ladle into bowls, sprinkle with parsley and mint, and serve with lemon wedges on the side.

Chestnut vendors on Taksim Square at night

Glossary

aşurelik buğday: peeled wheat
substitute: pearl barley

buğday: unpeeled wheat
substitute: pearl barley

bulgur: cracked wheat
substitute: couscous

çörek otu: black cumin seeds
substitute (at least visually):
poppy seeds

(tel) kadayıf: dried thin strings
of dough, also called angel's hair
Sadly, there's no equivalent to angel's
hair. Possibly glass noodles, but we
haven't tried that yet...

kaymak: clotted cream
substitute: double cream

köftelik bulgur: finely ground
cracked wheat
substitute: bread crumbs

nar ekşisi: sweet and sour pomegranate
syrup
substitute: a reduction of balsamic
vinegar
Tip: If you cannot find *nar ekşisi*,
combine grenadine syrup and lemon
juice or fresh pomegranate juice,
bring to a boil, and reduce until
syrupy; then stir in some lemon juice.

pekmez: grape molasses
substitute: sugar-beet molasses or syrup

pişmaniye: sesame cotton candy
substitute: regular cotton candy or
meringue

pul biber: red pepper flakes
substitute: mild ground paprika
Tip: *pul biber* is available in various
degrees of heat. We use the mild,
slightly sweet version.

salça: paprika paste
substitute: tomato paste plus mild paprika
and chili
Tip: There are two versions: *tatlı biber
salçasi* and *acı biber salçasi*. We use
the latter, which is hotter.

şehriye: orzo or other small pasta
that is added to rice
substitute: vermicelli

sucuk: garlic sausage(usually made
with beef or lamb)
substitute: chorizo

sumak: spice from the staghorn tree
substitute: grated lemon peel

süzme yoğurt: strained plain
whole-milk yogurt
substitute: labne

tahin: sesame paste
substitute: almond pulp
Tip: Don't store *tahin* in the fridge as it
gets too firm. Shake or stir before using.

tahin helva: crumbly, sweet paste made
from sesame seeds, honey, sugar, and oil.
We cannot think of a suitable substitute.
Helva is unique!

yoğurt: yogurt with at least 3.5% fat
substitute: yogurt with less fat or quark

yufka: paper-thin dough sheets
substitute: puff pastry

zeytin ezmesi: olive paste
substitute: *açma* makes a great pesto...
Tip: It's best to make olive paste yourself.
For a jar, mix 2 cups of chopped pitted
black olives with 3 Tbsp olive oil, 1
garlic clove, 1 tsp rosemary, 1 Tbsp sumac,
and 1 Tbsp thyme and blend well. Season
with salt, pepper, and a bit of lemon juice.

PRONUNCIATION

Turkish is usually pronounced the way
it's written. The ü is a bit tricky,
though. Here's a small selection to help
with pronunciation:

c = as in jungle
ç = as in chat
ğ = mute; lengthens the previous
  vowel a, i, o, u
h = as in hat
I = as in cousin
j = as in pleasure
r = as in pen
s = as in soccer
ş = as in shoe
y = as in yacht
z = as in zebra

DICTIONARY

Hello: **Merhaba**
Welcome (+ answer): **Hoş geldiniz
(Hoş bulduk)**
Goodbye: **Hoşçakal** (say when you leave) /
Güle güle (you say when you stay)

Yes: **Evet**
No: **Hayır**
Okay: **Tamam**

Thanks: **Teşekkürler / Çok merci** (in case
you can't remember the former)
You're welcome: **lütfen**

Excuse me (when calling the waiter or
waitress): **Bakar mısınız?**
The menu, please: **Menü, lütfen.**

What do you have for vegetarians?:
Vejetaryen bir şey var mı?
Do you have wine/beer?: **Şarap/bira var mı?**

I'm allergic to nuts/gluten/lactose:
Findik/gluten/laktoz alerjisi duyuyorum.

One portion, please: **Bir porsiyon, lütfen.**
Two portions, please: **Iki tane, lütfen.**

Spicy: **Acı**
Not spicy - **Acısız**

Enjoy your meal: **Afiyet olsun**
Cheers: **Şerefe**

May you never lack anything (say this after
having had some tea.): **Ziyade olsun**

Compliments to the cook: **Eline sağlık**

Cafes, Shops & Online Sources

Ara Cafe
The Ara Cafe serves a yummy wheat salad
with pomegranate seeds (see page 43).
kafeara.com

Divan Pastanesi
Divan sells ginger *lokum*, our favorite.
divanpastaneleri.com.tr

Karaköy Lokantası
Isabel's spot for delicious meze,
especially *fava* (white bean purée):
karakoylokantasi.com

Mehmet Efendi
You get particularly good coffee powder
for *türk lahvesi* (Turkish coffee) at
Mehmet Efendi.
mehmetefendi.com

Paşabahçe
A good source for beautiful tea glasses.
pasabahce.com.tr

Saray
A chain of popular pudding shops.
saraymuhallebicisi.com

Online Sources

For help finding green walnuts:
localharvest.org
specialtyproduce.com
walnuts.us

For Turkish ingredients:
alibaba-shop.com
bestturkishfood.com
istanbulfoodbazaar.com
tulumba.com

Teşekkürler! Thank you!

Isabel thanks:
The busy test chefs Florian, Sonja, Eva, Sarah, Ekki, Carl, Bianca, and Andrea. Mom, Pops, the elves, Markus, Anne, Benjamin, Nicole, Greta, Emil, and Pepe for critical eating. Anne for the loan of the peppermills, Kürsat for his help. Fred for just about everything. Zoé for joining in.

Lisa thanks:
"Papa" Yüksel and Gülseli "Rosegarden," who introduced me to Turkish food early on. Elisabeth, Till, Christoph, Tim, Erkin, Simon, Broos, and Manu for holding still and eating. Lisa for her critical eyes and ears. Pauline and Sophie for their support at the start. Nelly for folding countless *mantı*. Tjade for energy. Freerk, Freerk, and Freerk for everything!

Veronika thanks:
Ayla for sharing her experience and her washing-up mountains with us. Gökçe for "Can you say that?" Yilmaz for his knowledge of fish. Sonar and Anna for moral support. The kids for eating it all.

We all thank:
… everyone who helped make this book what it is! Our Istanbul specialists Alparslan, Elif, Ayla, Senem, and Suphi for their culinary views of the city. Frederic for the wonderful pictures. Soner for nonstop eating of leftovers and amazing knowledge of Turkish cuisine. Brigitte Hamerski for her eagle-eye for detail. Nina Schnackenbeck for her open eyes and ears and much enthusiasm.

Istanbul the beautiful for its bustle and energy, boundless and inexpensive inspiration, and its endless supply of çay.

Writer and photo blogger **Isabel Lezmi** (right) loves fine words and delicious experiments, owns many more cookbooks than other books, turns her living space into a supper club, visits foreign supermarkets like other people visit museums, and buys seasoning rather than shoes. Istanbul is just as much home for her as Cologne, and if you ask nicely, she'll give you a culinary tour through the beautiful city on the Bosporus. *lecker-lezmi.com*

Lisa Rienermann (middle) is an illustrator, photographer, art director, and author. She tells stories with her pictures, and plays happily with food. She loves voyages of discovery, and loves to dream up projects in which, with interesting colleagues, she can put all this into play. She makes statistics out of waffles, pictures out of spilled fat or letters out of urban canyons. Her work is published internationally. *lisarienermann.com*

Veronika Helvacıoğlu (left) lost her heart in and to Istanbul. The Heidelberg native has lived in Istanbul for more than ten years. When she's not beautifying the locals as a make-up artist, she scouts exclusive film locations or designs carpets for her label *samimi*. With Isabel she started "süperstreusel," a pop-up bakery in Istanbul. *samimi-istanbul.com*

Recipe Index

weldon**owen**

Published in North America by Weldon Owen
1045 Sansome Street, San Francisco, CA 94111
www.weldonowen.com
Weldon Owen is a division of Bonnier Publishing USA

This edition published in 2017

Copyright© 2015 Edel Germany GmbH
Neumühlen 17, 22763 Hamburg
www.edel.com
Second edition 2015

Text and recipes: Isabel Lezmi
English Translation: Nina Schnackenbeck

Photography credits:
All photos: Lisa Rienermann,
except for photographs of Istanbul and portraits: Frederic Lezmi

Printed in China

Library of Congress Cataloging-in-Publication data is available

10 9 8 7 6 5 4 3 2 1
2017 2018 2019 2020

ISBN 978-1-68188-220-8